Caravaggio

Cover
Boy with a Basket of Fruit, *detail,*
1593-1594. Galleria Borghese, Rome.

Text by Stefano Zuffi

Translation by Huw Evans

Photograph Credits
Electa Archives, Milan
Scala, Florence

Printed in Italy
© 1997 by **Electa**, Milan
Elemond Editori Associati
All Rights Reserved

This volume was printed by Elemond S.p.a.
at the plant in Martellago (Venice) in 1997

Caravaggio

Electa/Art Books International

Caravaggio

The development of art usually follows a patient and gradual path. It is only in a few, very rare cases that a master has proposed, right from his very earliest work, a fundamental renewal, involving a sudden break in the smooth succession of figurative expressions. Among these "revolutionaries" Caravaggio occupies an exceptional position. An enormous gulf separates the conception of his paintings from that of his contemporaries, as is demonstrated by the heated critical debate that they provoked, by the number and quality of his disciples, and by the immediate interest and even the misrepresentations and negative consequences aroused by the artist's controversial masterpieces.

To the restrained, stilted exercises of late Roman mannerism and the cultural eclecticism of the Bolognese academics, Caravaggio opposed the emotional impact of a vision drawn from "life," that is from direct observation of the real world. This effect was obtained by means of two innovations: the unprecedented use of light and the reversal of the observer's role in the picture. Luminous diagonals—growing ever narrower as the painter aged—run across his canvases, and bring to light only a small selection of details, a terse and highly expressive gleaning. In addition, in front of one of Caravaggio's works, we are no longer "just" external spectators faced with a painted image, but feel ourselves to be eyewitnesses to a real event that is taking place, right in front of our eyes, at this very moment.

In spite of the memorable research carried out by Roberto Longhi into the "precedents" of Caravaggio, these radically new features, so powerful that they immediately came to represent "points of no return" for art, remain the independent and highly personal achievement of one

Self-portrait, detail of the *Martyrdom of Saint Matthew*. San Luigi dei Francesi, Rome.

of the most unpredictable talents in the history of painting.

The story of Caravaggio's life is concentrated within the two decades straddling the year of 1600. On the one hand, the romantic biography of a young painter, rich in dramatic and even tragic episodes, a prototype of the misfortunes of the "doomed artist"; on the other, the troubled and seething environment of Rome, in the years of Pope Sixtus V's "Renovatio Urbis." Caravaggio lived and worked in a city that had just regained its role as a meeting point for the most diverse expressions of artistic culture. In February 1564, shortly after the conclusion of the Council of Trent, Michelangelo had died. Just a month previously, Daniele da Volterra had been given the job of putting "breeches" on the nudes of the *Last Judgement*. The next thirty years saw the architects and artists of Rome hard at work on translating the dictates of the Council and the indications of the new religious orders, such as the Jesuits, into visual terms. The result was the imposition of a severe, ossified cultural model: a refined, impersonal art that Federico Zeri has defined as "timeless." Yet alongside the cold efforts of Scipione Pulzone, the Zuccari brothers, Gerolamo Muziano, and the Cavalier d'Arpino (who was to become Caravaggio's teacher), there were still the great examples of ancient and modern classicism: important statues and monuments of antiquity that had recently been discovered, the frescoes from the first twenty years of the century such as Raphael's *Stanze* and Michelangelo's ceiling in the Sistine Chapel. These were the great works of art that inspired the Bolognese painter Annibale Carracci, who was working in Rome in the same years as Caravaggio, as he pointed out the way for a return to classicism through academic teaching.

Annibale Carracci reached this point at the conclusion of a long and personal process of elaboration, involving a passionate reinterpretation of Correggio and the painters of the Veneto Cinquecento in a naturalistic key.

Caravaggio was certainly not the only painter from the north to make his way down to Rome on the eve of the seventeenth century: masters and apprentices from France, Flanders, Spain, the Netherlands, and Germany, each brought with him a store of his own artistic tradition, making the Eternal City into a great international crossroads. Alongside the sumptuous decorative art of the Baroque emerged the "genre" paintings: landscapes, still lifes, scenes from daily life.

Caravaggio entered this debate with all the polemical energy of a protagonist and was inevitably the cause of scandal. The echo of his works soon spread throughout Europe, and gave rise to one of the principal currents of the Seicento. But the decisive role played by Caravaggio did not come to an end in the seventeenth century. His influence reaches down to the present day (working perhaps through new means for the reproduction of images, such as photography or the cinema), an inexhaustible source of emotion and the highly modern intuition of a different way of seeing and "living" the work of art: no longer just with the mind and the eyes, but also with the rapacious, piercing, and gentle force of the feelings.

Youth in Milan and the Early, Difficult Years in Rome (circa 1571-1595)

Whole romances have been built around the life of Caravaggio: there are at least five biographies written by his contemporaries, with such a wealth of picaresque detail that they constitute true cloak and dagger adventures. In recent times, they have even inspired television and film versions. An ill-starred life and extraor-

Cardsharpers, 1594-1595. Kimbell Art Museum, Fort Worth (Texas).

dinary works have come together to create the figure of a fascinating artist. Yet (and perhaps as a direct result of these fanciful distortions), a number of questions relating to chronology and attribution still persist.

The first of all concerns the date of his birth. The artist's real name was Michelangelo, and he was the son of the architect Fermo Merisi. The nickname dates from his years in Rome, and derives from the small town of Caravaggio, between Milan and Bergamo, from which the painter's family came, although he himself was born in Milan (according to the most recent reconstructions), toward the end of 1571.

In the years of his adolescence in Milan, Michelangelo Merisi received his early training as an artist from Simone Peterzano, a painter of moderate talent. The promising young apprentice spent four or five years with his first master (engaged in a number of demanding and ambitious undertakings, such as the frescoes in San Maurizio and the Charterhouse at Garegnano), absorbing a twofold tradition. On the one hand, he followed the current of Lombard "realism" that, shortly before the middle of the sixteenth century, had found its most illustrious exponents in the Brescian painters Savoldo, Romanino, and Moretto; on the other, he got to know the work of the great masters of the Renaissance in Veneto.

In Milan Caravaggio was able to study one of Titian's masterpieces, the *Crowning with Thorns* now in the Louvre, that was destined to leave an indelible mark on his understanding and representation of dramatic moments in the Passion of Christ or the martyrdom of the saints. It is likely, moreover, that Peterzano had taken his young pupil with him on the occasional visit to Venice, where he may even have introduced him to the seventy-year-old, but still very active Tintoretto. Understandably, no works from the Milanese period, spanning Merisi's fourteenth to nineteenth years, have come down to us. Thus we cannot do more than reconstruct *a posteriori* the experiences and influences at work on the painter prior to his permanent move to Rome, at around the age of twenty.

His first few years in the city were difficult, not to say dramatic: his limited means, violent character, and fragile health did not help him to fit into an exacting and haughty artistic environment. The young man from Lombardy went through a quick succession of relationships with different painters. After an early period spent with the obscure and coarse Lorenzo Siciliano, and a subsequent contact with the elegant Antiveduto Gramatica, Caravaggio passed a longer period of time with Giuseppe Cesari, known as the Cavalier d'Arpino. In the studio of this "fashionable" artist, he distinguished himself as a specialist in the painting of flowers and fruit. Years spent in the humble work of an apprentice and in poverty: a touching testimony to this is provided by one of his earliest surviving works, the *Sick Bacchus* in the Galleria Borghese in Rome (Plate 1). Dating from around 1591, it is a symbolic self-portrait made at the time of his hospitalization as the result of an attack of malaria.

Represented largely by apocryphal works and copies, some of which have preserved the memory of lost originals, his activity in the early years of his stay in Rome was mainly of the "genre" kind: no sacred, historical, or mythological scenes, but people engaged in everyday tasks that often served as the starting point for acute psychological observations, such as the *Boy Bitten by a Lizard* in the Fondazione Longhi in Florence (Plates 2, 3), or the pretext for stupendous still lifes, such as the *Boy with a Basket of Fruit* (Plate 5) in the Galleria Borghese and the *Bacchus* in the Galleria degli Uffizi (Plate 4).

In his early paintings Caravaggio revealed his links with the Lombard tradition through somewhat affected references to the naturalism of Savoldo. Having laboriously achieved a measure of independence, he then showed a predilection for themes taken from folklore (as can be seen in canvases like the *Cardsharpers* and the *Good Fortune* [Plate 6], of which numerous versions are known), and musical subjects: the *Musicians* in the Metropolitan Museum in New York and the very fine *Lute Player* in The Hermitage (Plate 7) were the prelude to the enchanting angel playing a violin in the *Rest on the Flight into Egypt* in the Galleria Doria-Pamphili in Rome (circa 1594, Plates 9, 10). Like the *Sacrifice of Isaac* in the Uffizi, from around the same time, it is a limpid example of Caravaggio's ability to translate sacred scenes into terms of spontaneous realism.

This facet of the painter's work has been interpreted in two completely opposite ways: was it proof of a profound and "modern" devotion along the lines laid down by the Council of Trent or, on the contrary, an expression of his desire to render sacred themes vulgar? Viewed in this way, some of Caravaggio's works aroused a great deal of perplexity, and were even rejected by the people who had commissioned them.

A typical example of Caravaggio's approach is provided by the *Magdalen* in the Galleria Doria-Pamphili, a girl of the common people caught in the intimacy of her own room, transformed by a few touches into the prostitute in the act of repentance as described in the gospels. Thanks to his subtle rendering of light, to the accurately described details, and to the refinement of the "still life" that found its way into almost every canvas (with a virtuoso preference for transparent bottles half-filled with water), Caravaggio finally "made a name for himself." After five years of wretched existence, spent in penury, bizarre friendships, sordid rented rooms, and shady taverns, in about 1595, the still youthful painter from Lombardy gained the favor of a great patron, Cardinal Francesco Del Monte, who gave him lodging in his own palace and commissioned several canvases from him, raising him from a state of poverty to the rank of one of the most prominent artists in Rome.

However, notwithstanding the honors and comforts, Caravaggio was never to renounce his "wild" life, violent and dissolute in the extreme.

Fame, Fall, and Flight:
Ten Crucial Years (1596-1606)

The *Still Life with a Basket of Fruit* (Plate 12) has been in the Pinacoteca Ambrosiana ever since its foundation, for it had been given to Federico Borromeo by Cardinal Del Monte. It is the only true "still life" that is acknowledged by all experts to be the work of Caravaggio (1596). It was painted at a time when this particular genre of art was in its infancy, and Caravaggio was to leave an indelible mark on it: the worm boring its way into the apple, at the center of the composition, transforms a virtuoso display of imitative skill into a work of touching realism, into which is insinuated a sense of the passing of time, of the way in which things are corroded as it passes, starting them on the path to their inevitable decay.

In pictures like this, painted toward the beginning of his stay with Cardinal Del Monte, Caravaggio seems to be showing a desire to linger over moments of quiet meditation, always imbued with a touch of thoughtful melancholy. In this period he produced such noble and austere canvases as the *Saint Catherine of Alexandria* in the Thyssen-Bornemisza Collection, the *David and Goliath* in the Prado, and the *Narcissus* in the Galleria Nazionale d'Arte Antica in Rome. Even in paintings of more dynamic subjects the attitudes and expressions seem to be frozen: typical examples are the *Judith and Holofernes* also in Rome's Galleria Nazionale d'Arte Antica (Plate 8) and the *Head of the Medusa* in the Uffizi (Plate 11). As is apparent, the theme of decapitation was a favorite of Caravaggio's, and was to reappear, always accompanied by effects of high tragedy, in his later works.

The *Supper at Emmaus* in the National Gallery in London (circa 1598, Plate 13), in which the basket of fruit in the foreground is an explicit reference to the *Still Life with a Basket of Fruit* in the Pinacoteca Ambrosiana, is the work that brings this period of Caravaggio's career to a close. In the picture in London the attitudes are again contained and calm, the atmosphere one of profound but serene lyricism. However the closer we get to 1600 the dimmer the light grows, or at least the more sharply directed and less diffuse. No less refined in its details, the Dionysiac *Amor Vincit Omnia* in the Staatliche Museen of Berlin (Plate 14) already heralds a new period, filled with outbursts of emotion and new tensions.

Engagements and commissions of great importance now followed in quick succession. In 1599, at the end of a series of exhausting disputes, Caravaggio was given the task of painting three scenes from the life of Saint Matthew in the Contarelli Chapel in San Luigi dei Francesi. The work encountered considerable difficul-

First version of *Saint Matthew and the Angel*, destroyed in the fire in the Berlin Museum, 1945.

Portrait of a Knight of Malta. Palazzo Pitti, Florence.

ties (radiographs have revealed the extent to which Caravaggio studied and modified the compositions of the two lateral scenes; the first version of the altar painting was rejected by the canons, and was lost in the fire at the Berlin museum in 1945), but the eventual result has proved to be decisive for the history of art.

The *Martyrdom of Saint Matthew* (Plates 15, 16) presents us a Caravaggio not yet wholly liberated from the strictures of late mannerist composition, as can be seen from the majestic nudes in the foreground. On the other hand, and violent irruption of the murderer, the body of Saint Matthew hurled to the ground in an impossible attempt at defense, and the cry of terror loosed by the altar boy are all inventions of absolute novelty.

Caravaggio displays his mastery of light, with flickering gleams that play over the fleeing congregation, amongst whom the self-portrait of the artist can be recognized. These groups of figures are reminiscent of Raphael's *Transfiguration* and Leonardo's *Last Supper*, but the artist has skillfully reworked them to his own ends. The *Calling of Saint Matthew* (Plates 17, 18) turns entirely on the passing of a moment of time over a ray of light: the figure of Christ (half hidden by Saint Peter), who is pointing to Saint Matthew at the tax collector's table, is counterbalanced by the group of seated gamblers, a much imitated but unequalled example of the composition of bodies facing one another. Its details are carefully studied and yet the whole remains extremely natural, sustained by an impeccable technique and a keen feeling for portraiture. The brightly lit dust and the presence of young men with feathered caps led the artist's contemporaries to compare this work with the paintings of Giorgione, a parallel with no particular foundation yet one that has persisted for a long time in criticism of Caravaggio's work.

The first version of *Saint Matthew and the Angel* was "taken down by the priests, who said that that figure had no decorum nor the appearance of a Saint, sitting there with his legs crossed and his feet rudely exposed to the people. Caravaggio was in despair at this affront" (Bellori). The picture now on the altar (Plates 19, 20) dates from 1602 and is still based on the relationship between the pose of the angel and that of Saint Matthew, precariously balanced on a rickety stool: once again an image captured at a moment in time, through the flash of glances and the correspondence of actions.

Before completing this work, Caravaggio carried out a second prestigious commission, received immediately after the one for the Contarelli paintings: two canvases for Cardinal Cerasi in Santa Maria del Popolo. Out of this came, between 1600 and 1601, the *Crucifixion of Saint Peter* (Plate 21) and the *Calling of Saint Paul* (Plate 22). Both scenes, rich in pathos, are set in an atmosphere of solitude and silence. Eliminating any hagiographic reference, Caravaggio interprets the fate of the two saints as simply human events. Saint Peter's executioners are tired, worn out by the exertions of a hard job, and do not appear brutal and violent as in the assassination of Saint Matthew. Saint Paul does not have his vision on the road to Damascus, but in the gloom of the stables, the only witnesses the stableman and the great dappled horse, which almost turns into the true protagonist of the scene.

Caravaggio's life, from 1601 onward, was a long series of brawls, injuries, rowdy nights, robberies, libel actions, and arrests, culminating in a murder, perhaps unintentional, during a fight of four against four over a game of racquets. An increasingly dissolute life, that seemed to spur him on to an exaggerated, expressionistic interpretation of the subjects he painted. And yet, having passed the age of thirty, Caravaggio felt the desire to try his hand at a "classic" theme, painting the *Entombment* (Plates 23, 24) for Santa Maria in Vallicella (now in the Pinacoteca Vaticana). The picture is composed around a solid group of figures, imbued with a dignified sorrow. The pyramidal structure and the robust nude figure of Christ have suggested a reinterpretation of the works of Michelangelo, filtered through the unmistakably "Lombard" feeling for light, here treated as a motionless and diffuse reflection. There is also a hint of classicism in the pose of the *Madonna dei Pellegrini*, or *Madonna di Loreto*, in Sant'Agostino (Plates 25, 26), which was painted between 1603 and 1605. To the unaffected elegance of the woman standing on the threshold of her house, with the Child wrapped in deep shadow, Caravaggio contrasts the ruffled figures of the two poor wayfarers on their knees, dirty and clothed in rags, anticipating by more than a century the "vagabonds" of Ceruti. At the very time that Annibale Carracci was putting the finishing touches to the ceiling of the Palazzo Farnese, the deliberate manifesto of a renewal of classicism, a heated debate was developing around Caravaggio. His works, undoubtedly, were powerful and realistic, but they lacked "decorum" and did not conform to the rules of "great painting." The feeling of perplexity was only increased by the nudity of the Christ child in the *Madonna dei Palafrenieri*, formerly in St. Peter's and then removed and acquired by Cardinal Scipione Borghese for the Gallery in which it still hangs.

During the first few months of 1606 Caravaggio's fortunes in Rome went into steep decline. The Discalced Carmelites of the church of Santa Maria della Scala rejected the *Death of the Virgin* (bought by Rubens on behalf of the Gonzaga, after a series of vicissitudes it ended up in the Louvre, Plate 28). This, the last of Caravaggio's masterpieces painted in Rome, was considered unseemly because of the attitude of the Madonna, and perhaps also because of the model used by the painter, whom, it appears, was a well-known prostitute. In contrast with the *Entombment* in the Pinacoateca Vaticana (Plates 23, 24), painted about three years earlier, Caravaggio refrained from any hint of rhetoric and created an agonizing scene, of dignified poverty, dominated by the great blood-red drape at the top.

Almost simultaneously with this professional humiliation, another event brought the painter's stay in Rome to an abrupt end. At the end of May, during a fight that broke out for pointless motives, Caravaggio was wounded, but in turn killed one of his opponents.

Sought by the authorities, he fled hastily, under the protection of the Princes Colonna, who "covered his escape" and offered him shelter in their residences at Palestrina and Zagarolo. Here the exile painted the *Supper at Emmaus* now in the Pinacoteca di Brera (Plate 27). The table has been cleared of the food with which it was covered in the earlier painting of the same subject, now in London (Plate 13). All that is left as a reminder of Caravaggio's skill with the "still life" is an earthenware water jug. The painter's concentration is now exclusively on the human figures, which emerge from the shadows with all the deeply felt inner charge of their passionate feelings. In this case the identification of the diagonal blade of light is extremely evident, and betokens the last phase in the life and career of Caravaggio, spent in the south in the longing and hope that he would be able to return, one day, to Rome.

The Odyssey over the Sea and along the Beaches of his Final Years (1606-1610)

Caravaggio spent the years of 1606 and 1607 in Naples, the great Mediterranean capital which was nearly at the peak of its contradictory splendor. While his friends and patrons pulled strings to obtain a pardon, the painter worked industriously. Not all the works recorded in the sources have survived, but those that have come down to us reveal the compositional ardor, the popular animation of Caravaggio's early period in Naples. The *Madonna of the Rosary* is now in Vienna, at the Kunsthistorisches Museum (Plate 29), and has had a curious history: it is even possible that the painting was begun in Rome and finished in Naples. The altarpiece is thronged with notables and commoners, all mingled together, while the Dominicans act as intermediaries with the Madonna: on the left, the client is portrayed facing the observer, and is an example of Caravaggio's problematic portraiture. His only indisputable portrait was burned in the Berlin museum, and none of the others that have been attributed to him, some of which are extremely interesting, are accepted by all the experts.

The large canvas depicting the *Seven Acts of Mercy* now in the Gallerie di Capodimonte (Plates 30, 31) is the most complex of Caravaggio's works in Naples. The painter had the powerful idea of placing the Madonna as if on a stage made out of angels: from this position, leaning forward, she is able to see a tumultuous but real scene, painted from the viewpoint of the corner of the alleys in the Spanish Quarters. The acts of mercy are represented all together, without a break, with great originality of technique and composition.

The *Flagellation*, painted for the church

Ottavio Leoni, *Portrait of Caravaggio*. Biblioteca Marucelliana, Florence. The drawing brings out the artist's aggressive personality.

of San Domenico Maggiore and now in the Gallerie di Capodimonte (Plates 32, 33), is probably Caravaggio's last Neapolitan altarpiece, and sets a dramatic seal to his whole career. Around the brightly lit torso of Christ bound to the column, his persecutors, slipping in and out of the shadows, are organizing an apparently endless series of torments. The modeling of anatomy is robust and corporeal, as in all of the painter's "southern" works.

In 1608 Caravaggio went on to Malta where, on 14 July, the Grand Master Alof de Wignacourt made him a Knight of the Order of Saint John. It was a great honor, and amounted to a sort of "rehabilitation." During the months he spent on Malta, the painter from Lombardy produced other works of great significance, and in particular, for the Cathedral of La Valletta, his largest canvas and the only one he ever signed (in the trickle of blood that flows from the severed head of Saint John): the *Beheading of Saint John the Baptist* (Plate 34).

Less than ten years after he painted the swirling composition of the *Martyrdom of Saint Matthew* (Plates 15, 16), Caravaggio approached the scene in a totally different way: a bare and dismal setting, the courtyard of a prison, forms the background to the few figures of the decapitation. Amidst horror, piety, and the cold execution of a sentence, the drama is enacted in an icy silence. Brilliant color, used for the last time in the *Madonna of the Rosary* (Plate 29), has now been completely dispensed with. Almost the whole of the right-hand side of the picture is basically empty, and is an anticipation of the experimental use of space in the works he painted in Sicily.

However his stay on Malta did not last long: in October the true reason for his flight from Rome was discovered and the painter was summoned to appear before the court. Caravaggio fled once again to Sicily. Pursued in vain by sea, he was ignominiously expelled from the Order of Saint John.

Landing at Syracuse, he devoted himself to archeological explorations (during one of which he baptized the celebrated stone quarry near the Greek Theater as the "Ear of Dionysius") and painted the *Burial of Saint Lucy* for the church of Santa Lucia. Like his other Sicilian works, the canvas is not in a good state of preservation, and yet it clearly reveals the new direction in which the painter was moving. All the figures, gathered around the body of the saint, seem to be crushed by the wall that looms behind them, an enormous and empty space that towers heavily over the group.

After his move to Messina in 1609, Caravaggio confirmed this tendency to leave vast areas of the composition free in two canvases, both now in the Museo Nazionale: the *Raising of Lazarus* and the *Adoration of the Shepherds* (Plate 35).

The theme of the Crib returns in the *Nativity with Saints Lawrence and Francis* (Plate 36). This was formerly in the Oratory of San Lorenzo in Palermo, but it was stolen in 1969 and has never been recovered. It is feared that the beautiful canvas has been cut up into pieces to prevent its identification.

On 20 October 1609, a year after his flight from Malta, Caravaggio returned to Naples. A papal pardon seemed imminent, thanks to the intervention of Cardinal Gonzaga, but his misadventures were not over: the painter was attacked and stabbed at the door of the tavern where he was staying. The wound was so serious that rumors spread of his death. In reality, he had the energy to paint yet more masterpieces during the ten months he spent in Naples. He returned to the obsessive theme of the severed head, painting two versions of *Salome Receiving the Head of the Baptist* and a moving *David with the Head of Goliath* (Galleria Borghese, Plate 37), hinting, in the contorted features of the slain giant, at a final self-portrait.

The summer of 1610: the beach of Port' Ercole, a Spanish stronghold on the coast of the Italian mainland, provided the setting for the last act in the life of the painter, who had not yet reached the age of thirty-nine. It was from here that Caravaggio was waiting to depart for Rome, aboard a felucca, in the belief that his pardon was about to be granted. Instead, perhaps because of the scar from his recent wound, he was mistaken for someone else and imprisoned. Two days later, his true identity having been established, he rushed to the harbor, but the ship had already left, apparently with all his belongings still aboard. This is how Bellori tells the story of the last few hours of his life: "He could no longer find the felucca, so that flying into a rage, he ran frantically along that beach under the burning rays of the sun to see if he could catch sight of the vessel that carried his things out at sea. Eventually reaching a place on the beach he went to bed with a high fever, and without human aid died wretchedly within a few days, as wretchedly as he had in fact lived." It was 18 June 1610: his pardon and permission to return to Rome arrived, with derisive futility, on the 31st of the same month.

The Legacy

The Seicento truly began under the sign of Caravaggio: while the painter was still alive, a very fierce critical debate sprung up over his work, and almost all the artists of Europe, it can be said, began to show a great interest in it. Nor did Caravaggio's influence fade away, in spite of a number of factors that might have had a decidedly negative effect. In the first place, the Lombard painter had not created a proper school: in Rome he had worked in isolation, without apprentices or collaborators. Secondly, a number of his works were rejected by his clients.

Finally, around 1620, the refined classicism of the Bolognese school established itself definitively as the main Roman current. It should not be forgotten, moreover, that painters who were destined to become interpreters of "ideal beauty" such as Guido Reni and Guercino did in fact pass through a "Caravaggesque" phase. Scholars and critics of an academic bias pointed to Caravaggio as an example of how "not" to paint, drawing inspiration solely from nature without an adequate study from models. And the reason for this disapproval, inconceivable today, is in part to be sought in the "degeneration" of Caravaggio's art into a manner, an out-and-out method devised by the Cremonese painter Bartolomeo Manfredi that effectively turned Caravaggio's ideas into a facile and popular style. In this way the repetitive subjects were made more attractive for the "market," with results that end up a long way from Cara-

vaggio's original intentions: bald heads with knitted brows, "rakes" decked out in plumes, reflections in pewter and gleaming fruit crop up over and over again, in a variety of different combinations. On the other hand some artists, such as the Ticinese Giuseppe Serodine and the Dutch painters living in Rome, took Caravaggio's approach to the opposite extreme, producing pictures in which they appeared to be seeking to depict the filthy and the deformed at the cost of all else.

While Caravaggio's legacy was accepted only with difficulty in Rome, where it was long opposed by the critics (resulting in mistakes of attribution that are difficult to clear up), other cities quickly saw the birth of schools based on his work. The first of these was Naples, where the master had spent two distinct periods of his life: Battistello Caracciolo, the Spaniard Jusepe de Ribera, and Massimo Stanzione were just three of the principal exponents of a very lively circle, that included a large number of outstanding figures.

Orazio Gentileschi and Antiveduto Gramatica, both of Tuscan origin, offered a particularly subtle interpretation of Caravaggism, with a patina of noble melancholy, while the Venetian Carlo Saraceni and the Veronese Marcantonio Bassetti attempted—without a great deal of success—to transplant onto the soil of Veneto ideas of Caravaggio's that they had experienced and elaborated at first hand.

The Genovese school was one of the quickest to pick up the naturalistic bent and pictorial technique of Caravaggio: the Genovese were favored in this by the visits to their city of great Flemish painters like Rubens and Van Dyck, who can be considered the first non-Italian interpreters of Caravaggio at the highest level. During his long stay in Italy, Rubens got to know Merisi, copied his works, and purchased the *Death of the Virgin* (Plate 28) for the Dukes of Mantua. On his return to Antwerp, he applied Caravaggio's ideas to his own extremely personal art. Out of this came a Flemish current, soon to be flanked by a Dutch one, in part sustained by painters who came to Italy, in part entrusted to local masters. Its popular themes, favorites of the northern tradition, were handled with a new dignity and an intimate poetry: the work of Vermeer, Franz Hals, and Rembrandt himself is indebted to Caravaggio.

There was an even more direct connection between Italy, much of which was under Spanish dominion, and the painters of the Iberian peninsula. Apart from the case of Ribera, who became a citizen of Naples, great artists like Velazquez and Zurburán studied the Roman and Neapolitan output of the Lombard artist with attention and intelligence. Also, the French "Romanists" Valentin de Boulogne and Simon Vouet were direct heirs of the Caravaggesque experience. In essence, then, it can be said that the revolution brought about by Caravaggio exercised greater influence abroad than in Italy.

As far as the history of criticism is concerned, while Caravaggio remained at the center of a continual clash of favorable and antagonistic opinions throughout the seventeenth century, the eighteenth century appeared to ignore him altogether. Idealistic and neoclassical esthetics had no time for Merisi's passionate realism, who was for the most part interpreted in the light of the presumed "aberrations" of his less gifted successors. There was no real critical rehabilitation of his work even in the nineteenth century, even though many artists (such as Cézanne) took up Caravaggesque concepts, and the development of photography drew some of its inspiration from the ex-ample set by luminarism. On the other hand, the seventeenth century and everything covered by the term "baroque" have long suffered from an extreme prejudice, so blind that it has led to a wholesale underestimation of all forms of artistic expression subsequent to the mythicized Renaissance. We must be thankful to Italian criticism in particular for the timely reevaluation of the catalogue of Caravaggio's works, and for having pointed out the important role that he played on the threshold of the Seicento. In spite of their contrasting methods and results, great scholars like Roberto Longhi, Matteo Marangoni, and Lionello Venturi were the leading figures over some thirty years of research, culminating in a memorable anthological exhibition staged in Milan in 1951. That date marks the beginning of a new era in criticism. With the fundamental role played by Caravaggio in the history of art firmly established, the critics have moved on to the subtle interpretation of his religious themes, to the acceptance (not without argument) of new paintings as original works, and to the revision of the chronology. Among other things, it is only recently that his date of birth has been shifted back by about two years with respect to the undocumented tradition, which had been accepted by Longhi himself, setting it at 1573. Particular attention has been given to the proposed attribution of portraits and still lifes to the master.

Through studies, congresses, and international exhibitions, the effort is continuing to define with ever greater clarity the debt that the whole of seventeenth-century painting owes to this great Lombard painter who led such a dramatic and singular life.

1

1. Sick Bacchus, *1591-1593,*
canvas, 66 × 53 cm. Galleria
Borghese, Rome.
In the absence of paintings
attributable to Caravaggio's
adolescence, during the time he
was a pupil in Milan, this
canvas is considered to be the
oldest of his works known to us.
Given its weak and emaciated
appearance, the figure of
Bacchus is often seen as a
pathetic self-portrait painted at
the time of the young artist's
hospitalization for an attack
of malaria. On the other hand,
the slight twisting of the body
and the silvery tonality may be
an echo of his apprenticeship
under Simone Peterzano.

2

2, 3. Boy Bitten by a Lizard,
c. 1593, canvas, 66 × 39 cm.
Fondazione Longhi, Florence.
"That head appears to be really
shrieking and the whole was
worked with diligence."
Baglione's words draw attention
to two features of this juvenile
work, one of the earliest known
to us: the realistic way that the
expression of pain and
astonishment has been caught
in a flash (and which can be
related to Leonardo's
investigation of the "movements
of the mind") and the impeccable
precision of the still life, with the
characteristic glass bottle that
Caravaggio so often depicted at
the beginning of his Roman
period.

4

4. Bacchus, c. 1593, canvas,
95 × 85 cm. Galleria degli
Uffizi, Florence.
Rediscovered in an amazing
fashion and in a precarious state
by Longhi and Marangoni in
the storehouses of the Uffizi, the
canvas depicts a recurrent theme
in Caravaggio's early work, in
which he lavishes attention on
the details of flowers and fruit
but is already capable of
insinuating a vague air of
ambiguity beneath the heavy
eyelids and fleshy lips of this
young Bacchus, rendered torpid
and turbid by wine.

5

5. Boy with a Basket
of Fruit, *1593-1594,*
canvas, 70 × 67 cm.
Galleria Borghese, Rome.
It would be simplistic to regard
the "Fruit Seller" merely as the
last stage on the way to the Still
Life with a Basket of Fruit *in*
the Pinacoteca Ambrosiana
(Plate 12). It is really a quite
separate work, belonging
to the important group of
Caravaggio's early paintings
depicting ordinary people from

the alleys and taverns around
Piazza Navona.

6. The Good Fortune,
c. 1594, canvas, 99 × 131 cm.
Louvre, Paris.
This delightful canvas marks a
shift in the subjects portrayed by
Caravaggio from people taken
from the street to scenes from the
everyday life of the common
people. In this case, a young and
pretty gypsy, under the cover of
reading a gullible youth's hand,

is skillfully removing a ring
from his finger. According to his
seventeenth-century biographer
Bellori, in order to paint this
picture Caravaggio "hailed a
gypsy who was passing by chance
in the street, and taking her to
the inn portrayed her in the act
of fortune telling."
There is another version
of this composition, probably
also by Caravaggio himself,
in the Pinacoteca Capitolina
in Rome.

7

7. The Lute Player, *1594,
canvas, 94 × 119 cm. The
Hermitage, St. Petersburg.
Numerous works from the early
years in Rome are devoted to
musical subjects and at times,
as in this case, the notation is
perfectly legible; it has even been
possible to stage concerts with
music taken from Caravaggio's
compositions. Moreover, the lute
player in The Hermitage is*

*another example of
Caravaggio's juvenile style,
which can be traced back to the
precious luminarism of the
Brescian painters of the
Cinquecento, and to Savoldo
in particular.*

8

8. Judith and Holofernes,
*1595-1596, canvas,
144 × 195 cm. Galleria
Nazionale d'Arte Antica, Rome.
This spectacular and dramatic
scene belongs to a quite distinct
group of pictures, painted at the
beginning of his association with
Cardinal Del Monte, in which
the figures are given an
unusual sharpness, almost a
harshness (note, for example, the*
*face of the aged servant
accompanying Judith). A
uniform and unwavering light
brings out the most macabre
details: the theme of the severed
head and flowing blood is one
of the most frequent in
Caravaggio's work, and
represents a leitmotiv running
through almost every stage
of his career.*

9

9, 10. The Rest on the Flight into Egypt, *1594-1596, canvas, 130 × 160 cm. Galleria Doria-Pamphili, Rome. This painting marks the culmination of the painter's juvenile period, and seems to be a final homage rendered to the tradition of Lombard realism. The diffuse luminosity, the presence of the landscape (which was about to disappear from* Caravaggio's painting), and the extremely elegant angel playing a viola convey an atmosphere of rustic calm. Even when painting a sacred subject—and this picture is the first in which he does so in a complex manner—Caravaggio takes the same approach of accurate reproduction of nature as in his profane works.*

11

11. Head of the Medusa,
*c. 1596, canvas on oval shield,
diameters 60 × 55 cm.
Galleria degli Uffizi, Florence.
Commissioned by Cardinal Del
Monte, and sent by the latter as
a gift to the Grand Duke of
Tuscany as a sumptuous shield
for his ceremonial armor, this
is one of Caravaggio's more
curious works. While permitting
him to work on his favorite
theme of the severed head, it is
given an unusual and rhetorical
treatment here.*

12

12. Still Life with a Basket
of Fruit, *1596, canvas,
46 × 64 cm. Pinacoteca
Ambrosiana, Milan.*
*The picture is also known as the
"Fiscella" (Wicker Basket): this
is what it was called by Cardinal
Federico Borromeo, to whom Del
Monte sent it as a gift. It is said
that with this work Caravaggio
both initiated and brought to a*
*close the genre of the still life.
And, in effect, for the first time
a shabby and bare basket with a
few pieces of fruit in it is
elevated to the rank of absolute
protagonist of art, no longer an
"object" but a "subject." On the
other hand, in spite of the
subsequent popularity of still life
painting, in Italy and abroad,
the profound effect achieved by*
*Caravaggio has never been
matched. The worm working its
way into the apple at the center
of the composition conveys a
precise sense of the way that time
passes, eating deeply into things
and tainting their essence. Other
still lifes have been attributed to
Caravaggio, but none of them
has been unanimously accepted
by the critics.*

13

13. The Supper at Emmaus, 1596-1598, canvas, 139 × 195 cm. National Gallery, London. This is the first version of the Gospel subject that Caravaggio painted twice, at different stages of his career. Here, right at the end of his juvenile period, the still life on the table is still given considerable emphasis (with the reappearance, among other things, of a basket of fruit that closely resembles the one in the Ambrosiana).

On the other hand, the light is beginning to have a source, a precise angle, creating the gripping impression that the observer is in the real, physical presence of the figures in the picture.

14. Amor Vincit Omnia, 1598-1599, canvas, 154 × 110 cm. Staatliche Museen, Berlin. The alert and ambiguous figure of the youth is an example of the world of the back streets from which Caravaggio drew his models and ideas. The picture symbolizes the victory of love over the arts, represented by books and musical instruments scattered in picturesque disorder; it is yet another demonstration of the pains taken by Caravaggio in the painting of still lifes and of his liking for musical subjects.

15

15, 16. The Martyrdom of
Saint Matthew, *1599-1600,
canvas, 323 × 343 cm.
San Luigi dei Francesi,
Contarelli Chapel, Rome.*
*The set of three paintings in the
church of San Luigi dei
Francesi represents the largest
and most systematic commission
ever taken on by Caravaggio:
the solutions he proposes
(including the first version
of* Saint Matthew and the
Angel *and the retouches*

*revealed by radiography)
constitute an authentic
palimpsest, a "work in progress"
during which the painter
abandons the last vestiges of the
late Cinquecento (still to be seen
in the* Martyrdom*) and moves
on to a totally new form of
expression, characterized by the
subtle handling of light.*
The Martyrdom *is the most
crowded and dynamic scene,
centering on the bursting in of
the assassin and the wounded*

*saint: in the groups of figures
that are retreating in confusion,
Caravaggio produces a series of
expressions of great humanity,
culminating in the famous
image of the fleeing and
screaming altar boy.*
*Amidst skillfully rendered echoes
of Raphael and Leonardo,
Caravaggio has left his own
self-portrait in the man with
the short beard at the back,
immediately to the left
of the hired killer.*

17

17, 18. The Calling of Saint
Matthew, *1599-1600,*
canvas, 320 × 340 cm.
San Luigi dei Francesi,
Contarelli Chapel, Rome.
Embellished with penetrating
references to the painting of
the Veneto, the picture provides
an eloquent example of
Caravaggio's new and thrilling
use of light, no longer diffuse

but directed and slanting.
Christ, on the right, half
concealed by Saint Peter, is
turned toward Saint Matthew,
seated at the tax collector's table:
other figures form a ring, in a
pattern of contrasting poses and
very fine details. The
composition, which conveys a
very strong moral tension, has
been used as the basis for a long

series of pictures by the
"Caravaggesques."
For the most part, however,
it is the external, formal
characteristics of the painting
that they have imitated: thus the
group of soldiers with feathers
in their caps who are playing
dice was to become a
characteristic motif, inserted
into a variety of contexts.

19

19, 20. Saint Matthew and
the Angel, *1602, canvas,*
232 × 183 cm. San Luigi dei
Francesi, Contarelli Chapel,
Rome.
This is the second and definitive
version of the subject: the first
was rejected for its lack of
"decorum" in the portrayal
of Saint Matthew, and was
destroyed in the fire at the Berlin
museum in 1945. In the

surviving version, however, the
relationship between Saint
Matthew and the angel dictating
the Gospel remains very intense
and direct: a fervent exchange
of glances, a matching of
attitudes without intermediaries.
The natural pose of the saint is
an indication of the artist's
open-minded approach that the
scruples of his clients were
unable to shake.

21

21. The Crucifixion of Saint Peter, *1600-1601, canvas, 230 × 175 cm. Santa Maria del Popolo, Cerasi Chapel, Rome.*
The two canvases in the Cerasi Chapel were painted immediately after the series in San Luigi dei Francesi and represent a continuation of its ideas. *This depiction of Saint Peter's martyrdom shows how Caravaggio uses light to concentrate the gaze of the observer on a few figures, the true protagonists of the action.*
The sense of humanity and empathy is extended even to the jailers, who are not portrayed as brutal and cruel figures but as simple men, forced to do a difficult job.

22.

22. The Calling of Saint Paul
(Fall of Saint Paul,
Conversion of Saint Paul),
*1660-1601, canvas,
230 × 175 cm. Santa Maria
del Popolo, Cerasi Chapel,
Rome.*
*Caravaggio's totally free
interpretation of religious
subjects reaches one of its peaks*
*here: Saint Paul's vision does
not take place on the road
to Damascus, but in the semi-
darkness of a stable, dominated
by the dappled bulk of a large
horse, and is witnessed solely by
the stable hand, who stands out
from the shadows. The air of
silence and solitude enhances
the effectiveness of the scene.*
*In the contract for the execution
of the two pictures in the
Cerasi Chapel, Caravaggio
was described as "egregius in
Urbe pictor": notwithstanding
his frequent clashes with
the law, the artist, who had
not yet reached the age
of thirty, was at the height
of his fame.*

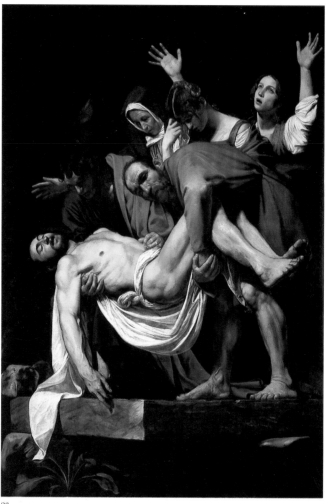

23

23, 24. The Entombment,
1602-1604, canvas,
300 × 203 cm.
Pinacoteca Vaticana, Rome.
Intended for Santa Maria in
Vallicella, this canvas is often
regarded as a sort of "classical
interlude" in the closing years
of Caravaggio's stay in Rome.
In fact the attempt to create an
impression of plasticity, worthy
of Michelangelo, is evident here:
the gestures are frozen in an
expressive manner and the light
lends three-dimensional form
to the figures.
On the other hand, there is
no lack of realism, of intense
suggestion, in the forward-
thrusting corner of stone
and the marked legs
of Nicodemus.

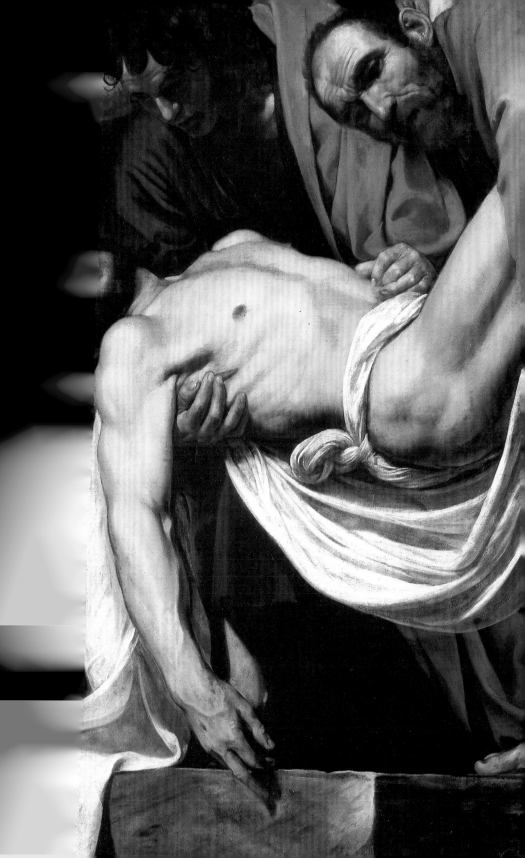

25

25, 26. Madonna dei
Pellegrini (Madonna
di Loreto), *1603-1605,
canvas, 250 × 150 cm.
Sant'Agostino, Rome.
The altar is dedicated to the
Madonna of Loreto, but
Caravaggio barely hints at the
cult of the Santa Casa, by*
*placing his Madonna
on the threshold of a house.
The scene is set in an
unassuming but highly
emotional atmosphere: Mary
herself is a simple woman,
remote from the traditional
iconography.
In front, the observer is*
*presented with the two figures
who have become almost the true
protagonists of the painting, the
poor, tattered, and filthy
pilgrims. It was the "close up"
of their dirty feet covered with
sores that caused such a scandal.*

*27. The Supper at Emmaus,
1606, canvas, 141 × 175 cm.
Pinacoteca di Brera, Milan.
It is a credible hypothesis that the
picture was painted while
Caravaggio was staying at the
residences of the Princes
Colonna, who gave him their
protection during his flight
from Rome to Naples. The
segmentation of space by the
light reinforces the mystical
suspension of the gestures and
the immediate, moving realism
of the picture. In comparison
with his early painting of the
same subject, now in London,
one notes the disappearance of
the rich and precious still life:
this time the table is bare and
mute, with a few objects that cast
deep shadows.*

27

29

28. The Death of the Virgin,
1606, canvas, 369 × 245 cm.
Louvre, Paris.
This is the last picture that
Caravaggio painted in Rome.
Intended for Santa Maria della
Scala, it was rejected by the
Carmelites because of its lack
of "decorum" and the suspicion
that the model used for the
Virgin was a prostitute drowned
in the Tiber. Acquired by the
Gonzaga on the advice of
Rubens, it then passed on to
King Charles I of England and
finally ended up in France. The
weeping apostles surround
Mary's cot, reinforcing the effect
created by the beam of light that
slants across the picture,
concluding with the figure
of Mary Magdalen in tears.
The rejection of this masterpiece
and the killing of Ranuccio
Tommasoni in a brawl, forced
Caravaggio to leave Rome
for good.

29. Madonna of the Rosary,
1606-1607, canvas,
364 × 249 cm. Kunsthistorisches
Museum, Vienna.

Probably painted for San
Domenico Maggiore in Naples,
this may be the first large canvas
from the painter's stay in
Naples. The composition, an
unusually crowded one, reveals
a taste for scenes of a complex
structure and filled with figures.
Unlike in the Roman works
(such as the Madonna di
Loreto), the faithful do not
appeal directly to the Virgin, but
to the Dominicans who act as
intermediaries. The figure on
the left, facing the observer,
is the client.

30

30, 31. **The Seven Acts**
of Mercy, *1607, canvas,*
390 × 260 cm. Church of the
Pio Monte della Misericordia,
Naples.
From the "balcony" formed out
of angels, the Madonna and
Child observe a scene of seething
activity. With brilliant intuition,
Caravaggio has set the episodes
alluding to corporal works
of mercy (feeding the hungry
and giving drink to the thirsty,
clothing the naked, succoring
pilgrims, healing the sick,
visiting prisoners, burying
the dead), in the streets of
Naples, using the light to pick
out the different devotional
groups.

32

32, 33. The Flagellation,
1606-1607, 286 × 213 cm.
Gallerie di Capodimonte,
Naples.
*The recent discovery of a
number of documents suggests
that this work dates from
Caravaggio's first period in
Naples, and not from the second
as, for stylistic reasons, Longhi
had supposed. In point of fact,
the bitter grief of this round
of torments, the shadows that
enfold the figures, and the
atmosphere of irremediable
tragedy are typical elements*

*of the last phase of the painter's
work.*

34. The Beheading of Saint
John the Baptist, *1608,
canvas, 361 × 520 cm.
Cathedral of Saint John,
La Valletta (Malta).
This is Caravaggio's largest
picture and the only one that he
signed (the painter's name is
traced with the blood that flows
from the stump of Saint John's
neck).
The evolution of Caravaggio's
poetics is reaching its final*

*stages: the artist, still a fugitive
and driven by the hope of
returning to Rome, has
completely abandoned the bright
colors and glowing details of
his youth. His attention is now
wholly concentrated on the use
of space: all the figures are
confined to the left-hand side,
while the entire right half of the
large Maltese canvas is occupied
by the blank wall of a prison,
giving the episode the chilling
atmosphere of a brutal
execution, carried out at the first
light of dawn.*

34

35

35. Adoration of the Shepherds, *1609, canvas, 314 × 211 cm. Museo Nazionale, Messina. While not in a good state of preservation, the canvas provides a demonstration of Caravaggio's determination to use space in completely new way. During his stay in Sicily the artist abandoned for good the bright colors of his youth in order to seek a more intense and expressive dialogue between the figures and the empty setting that surrounds them. He took a similar approach in the other picture preserved in Messina, depicting the* **Raising of Lazarus,** *and in the one of the* **Burial of Saint Lucy,** *painted for the church of Santa Lucia in Syracuse and now on permanent loan to the Museo Civico of the same city.*

36. Nativity with Saints Lawrence and Francis, *1609, canvas, 268 × 197 cm. Formerly in the Oratory of San Lorenzo, Palermo. This important picture was the best preserved testimony to Caravaggio's tortuous journey through Sicily in the penultimate year of his life: the canvases in Messina and Syracuse are in fairly poor condition. Unfortunately, the painting was stolen in 1969, and has never been recovered.*

37

37. David with the Head of Goliath, *1610, canvas, 125 × 100 cm. Galleria Borghese, Rome.*
Probably painted during the artist's second stay in Naples, this is one of his last works, and returns to the theme of the severed head. *In reality, it is also a reflection on the painter's own life, seeing that he was on the run from a sentence of capital punishment. The atmosphere of gloomy melancholy and bitter meditation and the way the paint is laid on with long, fibrous* brush strokes are typical features of Caravaggio's final works. *In the guise of the severed head of the vanquished giant, which bears more an expression of astonishment than of pain, we may recognize a final, anguished self-portrait.*

Where to See Caravaggio's Works

Caravaggio's work spans just two decades astride the year 1600; but this brief period sufficed him to initiate a far-reaching upheaval in the course of painting, embodied in about sixty surviving works. The Lombard painter's output falls into two periods separated by the turn of the century, when he painted the two canvases at the sides of the Contarini Chapel in the Church of San Luigi dei Francesi. From 1590 to 1600 his work consisted mainly of fairly small paintings of profane subjects or genre scenes for private collectors. Then from 1600 to 1610 Caravaggio mainly worked on altarpieces and large religious subjects to be displayed in public buildings. They were always oil paintings on canvas, with rare exceptions (the Uffizi *Medusa* is on a leather scroll; in the Casino Ludovisi in Rome there is a mural of *Jove, Neptune and Pluto*, but the attribution is disputed).

Not all his work has been preserved: a number of canvases, some of prime importance, are now lost: these are mainly youthful works recorded in older sources and some from the Neapolitan period; but in recent times there have also been serious losses, like the first version of *Saint Matthew and the Angel*, destroyed in the fire in the Berlin Museum in 1945, together with *Christ Waking the Apostles in the Garden of Gethsemane*. In 1969, the altarpiece of the *Nativity with Saint Francis and Saint Lawrence* was stolen from the Oratory of San Lorenzo in Palermo and has never been recovered. On the whole, however, Caravaggio's career as an artist is well documented and many of the most important works are still in their original locations. New attributions are not infrequent, some of them of the greatest interest, in particular concerning works in the United States.

After some decades in which the body of work attributed to Caravaggio remained stable (backed by Roberto Longhi's authoritative research), in recent years there has been a notable resurgence of studies in Italy and abroad. Exhibitions, publications, conventions, and sometimes remarkable discoveries (not always winning unanimous support among the critics) have extended the series of suggested attributions, sometimes with outstanding results. An example is the *Cardsharpers* at Fort Worth, a painting long sought-after by scholars. At the same time some famous works have been expunged from the catalogue: the best-known example is the fascinating *Narcissus* in Rome's Galleria Nazionale di Arte Antica, now attributed to a leading follower of Caravaggio, Giovan Battista called Spadarino.

Works in Italy

In his lifetime, Caravaggio divided collectors and art patrons. He won the favour of cultured, perceptive connoisseurs like Cardinal Del Monte and the *Marchese* Giustiniani, at the same time as some of his works were rejected as unworthy of the churches for which they had been commissioned. These contrasting attitudes are reflected in the distribution of his paintings in Italy and abroad. Rome, Naples and other Italian cities still have many of his more important works, but a sizeable number of paintings, including two altarpieces, have gone to foreign collections.

Rome

Caravaggio spent at least fifteen years of his working life in Rome: about a third of his surviving works are still in Roman churches and museums, many of them actually in the very churches and princely collections for which they were originally painted.

A visit should start with the latter works on the altars or side walls of churches and chapels. The most important cycle, a landmark of European seventeenth-century art, is in the Contarelli Chapel in the Church of San Luigi dei Francesi and was begun in 1599. On the altar is the second version of *Saint Matthew and the Angel*, while on the walls are the *Calling of Saint Matthew* and the *Martyrdom*, works that were decisive for their dramatic handling of light. Nearby are the paintings on the side walls of the Cerasi chapel in Santa Maria del Popolo, with the *Crucifixion of Saint Peter* and the *Calling of Saint Paul*.

In the church of Sant'Agostino there is a side altar devoted to the House of the Virgin at Loreto: it contains the moving *Madonna with Pilgrims*, expressing trepidation and conveying a firm sense of reality. The church of the Capuccini in Via Veneto contains the important but little-known *Saint Francis in Meditation*.

The Galleria Borghese is the essential starting point to see Caravaggio's works in Rome's museums: it contains the world's largest collection of his paintings, including what are probably the earliest and the latest of his surviving works, both—curiously—containing a self-portrait of the painter. The collection includes an altarpiece, the *Madonna dei Palafrenieri*, former-ly in St. Peter's, and some important youthful works: the *Sick Bacchus* and the *Boy with a Basket of Fruit*. A later work is *Saint Jerome*, while the moving *David with the Head of Goliath* and a thoughtful *Saint John* are regarded as among his last works. The collection also includes two *Still Lifes* attributed to Caravaggio by some scholars.

Also important is the series of works in the Galleria Dora Pamphili, which opens with the youthful masterpiece, the *Rest during the Flight into Egypt*. Also to be seen are *Mary Magdalen* and a version of *Saint John*.

The Vatican Gallery has a spectacular altarpiece, the *Deposition*, originally painted for Santa Maria della Vallicella. The National Gallery, housed in the Palazzo Barberini and Palazzo Corsini, has some important works as well as others of uncertain attribution. A masterpiece is *Judith and Holofernes*, flanked by a vigorous *Saint John the Baptist*. There are two works in the Pinacoteca Capitolina: the delightful *Good Fortune* and a sparkling *Saint John with the Lamb*. Finally one should see the great *Conversion of Saint Paul* in the Odescalchi Collection.

Naples

The sources mention a dozen or so works painted during his two sojourns in Naples, which proved a decisive influence on the development of the local school of painting. Today only three canvases remain: the *Martyrdom of Saint Ursula* in the collection of the Banca Commerciale and two masterpieces in the Gallerie di Capodimonte: the *Seven Works of Mercy* and the *Flagellation*.

Sicily and Malta

There remain significant traces of Caravaggio's visits to the Mediterranean islands.

The Museo Regionale of Messina possesses two dramatic paintings, still impressive despite the poor state of preservation: the *Adoration of the Shepherds* and the *Resurrection of Lazarus*. In Syracuse the church of Santa Lucia contains the *Burial of Saint Lucy*. La Valletta cathedral in Malta contains Caravaggio's largest painting, and the only one he signed: the *Beheading of John the Baptist*. It also has *Saint Jerome in Meditation*, recently recovered after being stolen.

Florence

There are a fair number of works by Caravaggio in Florentine museums. The Uffizi has the *Head of the Medusa*, the youthful *Bacchus* and the *Sacrifice of Isaac*, one of Caravaggio's few paintings with a landscape setting. The Galleria Palatina in Palazzo Pitti has a *Portrait of a Knight of Malta*, a precious example—hitherto little studied—of Caravaggio's work in portraiture, and the late *Sleeping Cupid*. The Fondazione Longhi has a version of the *Boy Bitten by a Lizard*. The Cassa di Risparmio of Prato possesses a *Flagellation of Christ* of uncertain attribution.

Other Italian Cities

Milan, the painter's native city, has two masterpieces: the *Supper at Emmaus* in the Pincacoteca di Brera and the celebrated *Basket of Fruit* in the Pinacoteca Ambrosiana.

Cremona's Museo Civico has the gloomy *Saint Francis in Meditation*.

Finally, the Galleria di Palazzo Rosso in Genoa has an important *Ecce Homo*.

Works Outside Italy

The relative rarity of Caravaggio's works means that museums outside Italy have few paintings, and this has sometimes led to attempts to flesh out collections by dubious attributions. The most significant works are the two altarpieces located in Paris and Vienna.

Vienna and Germany

The Kunsthistorisches Museum has the large *Madonna of the Rosary*, an outstanding work thronged with figures that was painted in Naples. It also contains an intense *David with the Head of Holofernes* and two works of doubtful attribution, the *Ascent of Calvary* and *Crown of Thorns*.

The Berlin Museum still contains a number of works, despite the disastrous fire of 1945: the *Victorious Cupid* is a masterpiece.

The Alte Pinakothek in Munich has an ambiguous *Lute-Player*. There is larger and richer interpretation of the same subject in the Hermitage Museum in St. Petersburg.

Paris

The Death of the Virgin in the Louvre is Caravaggio's most important painting outside Italy. After being painted in 1606 for Santa Maria della Scala in Rome, it was rejected by the church authorities and purchased by Rubens. The Louvre also has a version of the *Good Fortune* and a doubtful *Portrait of Alof de Wignacourt*.

The attribution of the *Flagellation* in the Rouen museum to Caravaggio is disputed.

London

There are three interesting works in the National Gallery: the first version of the *Supper at Emmaus*, a late *Salome with the Head of the Baptist* and a replica, recently acquired, of the *Boy Bitten by a Lizard*.

Madrid

The Prado contains two relatively small pictures on the theme of the severed head: *David Severing the Head of Goliath* and *Salome with the Head of the Baptist*.

The splendid painting of *Saint Catherine* is owned by the Thyssen-Bornemisza Collection in Spain.

The Toledo cathedral museum and the Monastery of Monserrat possess two different versions of *Saint John with the Lamb*.

United States

American museums are quite rich in works ascribed to Caravaggio, though in many cases the attribution is continually disputed.

The Metropolitan Museum of New York has an early *Group of Musicians*. There is a virile *Saint John the Baptist* in the Kansas City Museum. The Kimbell Art Museum in Fort Worth has the recently rediscovered the original version of the *Cardsharpers*, a painting previously known only through replicas. The very fine *Conversion of Mary Magdalen* may be a copy. The Wadsworth Athenaeum in Hartford possesses the finest version of the lyrical *Saint Francis Supported by an Angel*, a version of which is in the museum in Udine (Italy). Finally there is a *Still Life* in Washington's National Gallery.

Anthology of Comments

The words worthy man signify to me that he knows how to do his job well, as a worthy painter [is] one who knows how to paint well and imitate natural things well.

(From the record of Caravaggio's interrogation during the hearing of the action for defamation brought against him by the painter Giovanni Baglione, 28 August 1603)

There is also a Michelangelo da Caravaggio who does wonderful things in Rome... He has emerged out of poverty with great difficulty through constant work, seizing and accepting all, with astuteness and boldness, as do those who do not wish to be kept under through timidity and lack of daring... In addition, alongside the good grain there is the weed: in fact, he does not devote himself continuously to study, but when he has worked for a couple of weeks loafs around for a month or two, with his sword at his side and a servant in tow, and goes from one ball game to another, always ready to pick a quarrel and come to blows, so that one only sees him rarely. All this is not very like to our profession, for Mars and Minerva have never been great friends. Nonetheless, his painting is beyond dispute: it is executed with great elegance, is very pleasing, and is marvelously suited to providing an example to young painters.

(K. van Mander, *Het Schilder-boek*, 1604)

It is typical of this school [of Caravaggio] to illuminate with a single ray of light that comes from outside without reflections, as would be [the case] in a room with one window with the walls colored black, having the light and the shade very light and very dark, they come to give emphasis to the painting... In this way of operating this school is very observant of life, which it always keeps in front while it works; it works well with a single figure, but in the composition of historical scenes and the expression of feeling, depending this on the imagination and not on the observation of the thing, to portray the real life that they always keep in front [of them], it does not seem to me that they avail there, it being impossible to put in one room a multitude of men who represent the scene with that light from a single window, and have one who laughs or cries or pretends to walk or stays still to allow himself to be copied, and so then their figures, although they have strength, [are] lacking in movement and in emotions, in grace, that lies in that way of operating as will be recounted.

(G. Mancini, *Considerazioni sulla pittura*, 1619-21)

In the first chapel of the church of Sant'Agostino on the left hand side, he did a Madonna of Loreto portrayed from life with two pilgrims, one with muddy feet and the other with a torn and filthy bonnet; and for these trifles in respect of the parts having been painted in a great manner, an uproar was created by the common people.

(G. Baglione, *Le vite de' pittori*, 1642)

Endowed with particular talent [Caravaggio], wanting however the necessary

base of good drawing, he revealed himself then lacking in invention, and as if wholly devoid of idea of beauty, charm, decorum, architecture, perspective, and other similar proper fundamentals, which together render sufficient and worthy the true principal and greatest masters.
(F. Scannelli, *Il microcosmo della pittura*, 1657)

He painted a girl seated on a chair with her hands in her bosom, in the act of drying her hair; he portrayed her in a chamber, adding on the ground a pot of ointments with necklaces and jewels he made her out as Magdalen. Her face is turned a little to one side, and her cheek, neck, and breast is rendered in a pure, clear, and lifelike hue, accompanied by the simplicity of the whole figure, with the arms in a blouse and the yellow frock pulled back to the knee from the white petticoat of flowered damask. We have described this figure in detail to indicate his natural style and the imitation of realistic color in a few tints... Attracted by his style [many painters] embraced it willingly, since without other study and effort they eased the way to copy the natural, looking there for vulgar bodies without beauty. With the majesty of art thus treated by Caravaggio, each one gave himself leave, and the result was a contempt for beautiful things... Then began the imitation of base things, with the seeking out of filthiness and deformity, as some are wont to do most eagerly: if they have to paint a suit of armor, they select the most rusty, if a vase, they do not make it whole, but chipped and broken. Their

clothes are stockings, breeches, and caps, and so in imitating bodies, they dwell with all their care on the wrinkles and defects of the skin and outlines, making the fingers knotted, the limbs twisted by disease.
(G.P. Bellori, *Le vite de' pittori, scultori e architetti moderni*, 1672)

Guided by his dark and gloomy nature, he gave himself to the representation of objects with very little light, laying on the dark colors with a heavy hand. It seems as if his figures inhabit a prison that is lit poorly and from above. Thus his backgrounds are always gloomy, and the actors pose in a single plane, and there is hardly any degradation in his paintings; and nonetheless they delight for the great effect that results from that contrast of light and shade. It is no good seeking correctness of design or the choice of beauty in him. He used to laugh at the attempts of others to ennoble the expression of a face, or to find a beautiful arrangement of drapery, or to imitate a Greek statue: his beauty was something real.
(L. Lanzi, *Storia pittorica dell' Italia*, vol. I, 1795-96)

Caravaggio himself shows us all the false calculation of naturalism in a single head: this is the "Medusa" in the Uffizi. Always striving to convey the instant and therefore indifferent to the profound and immanent expression (that he achieves so well in the "Entombment"), he paints a woman's head at the moment of decapitation: but could not the same canvas have depicted the extraction of a tooth?

(J. Burckhardt, *Der Cicerone*, 1855)

As for the group on the right of the *Martyrdom of Saint Matthew*, I know of few works of art that state their stylistic intentions as clearly and forcefully as this one: where style is, I am tempted to say, reduced to a concrete and palpable thing. I recall few other figures in which the enormous vitality of a human body is rendered with simpler means than the nude of the executioner, where the highly original posture of the shoulder that rises above the bent body becoming its "head" and key, gives, in such a new and convincing way, the most effective and clear impression of the action... But the newest figure and the one that most breathes the air of the new times is that of the youth screaming as he flees: a new movement, indeed unique in its time, as an expression of *instantaneousness*, although still and fixed in the absoluteness of the new style, already wholly independent and mature in the wonderful head of the boy. That new style that, not to mention the Italians, Velazquez himself was to seize at once and, through him, was to reappear inevitably in the painting of more recent times.
(M. Marangoni, "Esperienze della mostra secentesca," in *Bollettino d'arte*, 1922)

In comparison with the grandiose and optimistic, but provisional, solution of the baroque, of which classicism already represented the beginning, Caravaggio's solution finds ... the mark of its own value, a bitterly realistic and perpetual one, in the definite and conclusive accord

between the physical and the metaphysical. And every authentic style contains within itself—or has done at least up until the beginning of this century—the dialectics of the dualism of nature and vision: extreme naturalness and extreme abstraction exchange places with one another. Thus in the abstract and impassable thicket of Caravaggesque chiaroscuro, where at first nothing is perceived except a tragic and primordial welter of light and shade, there emerges all of a sudden, and as if by fateful coincidence, an event that is the most realistic, the most tangible, in short the most natural that has ever been conceived and expressed. Here is the outcome and the conclusion of past developments in Lombardy and at the same time the beginning of new developments, not so much in Italy as in Europe, that through the restless and reeking slumber of the old giant of the baroque and without getting at all lost in those vapors, links up with the greatest achievements of modern times.
(R. Longhi, "Quesiti caravaggeschi: i precedenti," in *Me Pinxit*, 1927)

T he myth of the anti-classical painter, without masters, scorning the study of other artist's style, is rapidly fading. It was born out of the polemic accents of Caravaggio himself; but even if Caravaggio wanted people to think that he had no teachers but nature, he still looked with a penetrating gaze, and one capable of recollection at a distance of many years, at the works of Correggio, Raphael, Michelangelo, and Lorenzo Lotto.
He looked at the contempo-

rary work of Annibale Carracci and he looked at ancient sculptures. But only very detailed analysis has been able to reveal the storehouse of Caravaggesque culture, putting the lie to the legend of the uncultivated, primitive, and romantic painter.
On the other hand it is also true that this store of Caravaggesque culture was put into practice by a highly original artistic temperament, who not only selected the ideas for his compositions with the force of instinct, but often set to work on them with a polemic tone, wiping out the meaning that they had in the works of other artists, as is evident in his frequent references to Michelangelo, which are used to opposite ends. The lack of any original drawings by the artist himself, while it signifies, in the broader sense, that he did not give excessive importance to drawing in itself, does not exclude the possibility that he possessed notebooks (a very common practice among artists) in which he would jot down not only his "basic ideas" but also brief records of other people's works, something that would provide a better explanation of the references to the attitudes of figures and to schemes of composition, rather than to particular details of pictures.
(V. Mariani, "Caravaggio," in *Enciclopedia Universale dell'Arte*, vol. III, 1958).

C aravaggio abandoned the great compositional frameworks that had developed out of Renaissance schemes; he abandoned the conventions of the "historical painting" then in vogue, avoided the ideological scaffolding of the academies, and presented

in his works scenes of everyday life, conveying the plain and simple truth of their nature. A youth peeling a pear, a boy bitten by a lizard, a pair of cardsharpers, a girl drying her hair..., this is what Caravaggio proposes in contrast to pompous academic structures, simple motifs realized in equally simple and realistic forms; immediate motifs without the support of preparatory drawings, without the complicated elaboration of historical pictures, without a before and without an after: a painting recorded live, interested only in itself, in its own values, in its most intimate and secret truth.
(S. Bottari, *Caravaggio*, 1966)

H ow could a lad from Lombardy, an apprentice painter who arrived in Rome at the age of about eighteen, make himself, grow, overflow from the lowlying areas of Piazza Navona, across the Tiber, across the Alps, beyond the confines of his century and the following centuries, and come down to us as one of the greatest of mentors (perhaps the most enduring and effective of all), be adopted as the figurehead of the modern by the most disparate tendencies, the most contrasting factions? How is it possible that even today, after Kandinsky and Mondrian, the most casual passerby, or the most enthusiastic supporter of Pollock or Rauschenberg, or the most condescending advocate of art as play, on entering San Luigi dei Francesi feels an old wound opening in his breast that he thought had healed for good? They are questions without an answer, or whose only possible answer (despised by many) is that the

truth of a great creative passion is gauged by its duration, by its ability to serve as a fountainhead for ideologies, new convictions, and new styles: to reveal a new face, never seen before.
(R. Guttuso, "Antiaccademia," in *L'opera completa di Caravaggio*, edited by A. Ottino Della Chiesa, 1967)

Today it is hardly worth investigating the reasons for the rejection [of the *Death of the Virgin*]. Why did he "portray in the person of Our Lady a courtesan that he loved?" "Why with little decorum had he made the Madonna swollen and with bare legs," "having imitated too closely a swollen dead woman?"
In reality the picture seems to be telling how, in the squalid rented room, clumsily divided by a bloody drape hanging from the rafters of the ceiling and bare of any other furnishings apart from a cot, a chair, and a basin for wet cloths, the death of a local woman is mourned. Almost a scene from the doss-house. But the anguish of the onlookers seems to be given infinite meaning and authority by the devastating light that, shining from the left into the circle of already strangely glowing colors and yet struggling with every kind of shadow, lingers for a moment on the upturned face of the dead Madonna, on the crescent-shaped bald heads, throbbing necks, and emaciated hands of the apostles; it cuts right across the woeful face of John; it turns the seated and weeping Magdalen into a single luminous block; it makes her hand on her knee into a mere lump of clotted light.
(R. Longhi, *Caravaggio*, 1968 edition)

A painting by Caravaggio is composed in a different way to those by the other painters of his day, for whom the work was nothing but the staging of a theatrical event, or a thought, which implies that all its components should be visible to our gaze, in the space bounded by the frame. Caravaggio cuts a figure in half, as Albani complained: there is only just room for his Saint Paul in the *Conversion* in Santa Maria del Popolo, which is taken up by the great moonlit bulk of the horse, and these image shifts, these "close-ups," mean that the figures are no longer seen as parts of a story, but as actual beings, ready to emerge from the pictures and return to their places that will be, at one and the same time, those of earthly existence and of the transcendence with which the intense figures of great artists are endowed in our eyes. There is something, in Caravaggio's style, that always hints at these figures "outside the picture," in the ambiguity of the night, at once depressing and exalting, that his chiaroscuro calls to our attention.
(Y. Bonnefoy, "L'image et le tableau, dans la peinture du Seicento," in *Seicento. Le siècle de Caravage dans les collections françaises*, exhibition catalogue, 1988-89)

As far as the *Beheading of the Baptist* is concerned, Caravaggio's tragic identification with the decapitated Saint, already suggested by the way he signed his name with the red of his blood, can be better understood now, in the light of that "capital exile" whose anguish the painter bore in secret... The flickering light evokes the last tremor of life in the body of the

martyr, who has fallen face downwards, with his hands tied behind his back. The action is caught at its climax. The executioner, who has struck his blow with the sword, is now preparing to draw the blade with which he will finish severing the neck, delivering the "coup de grâce." The young woman (Salome) is impatiently holding out the platter on which the head will be placed, as indicated by the gesture of the warder, while the old woman reveals her horror and pity. The rope that hangs uselessly from the ring set in the wall, on the right-hand side, allows us to guess at what has happened just a moment previously, when the Saint was untied from that corner and dragged forward.
The relationship between space and figures has been modified with respect to that of his earlier paintings by increasing the amount of empty space, immersed in a mute half-light, that dramatizes the tonalities of a Titian in an uncertain and sunken inflection. The bodies have lost all their plasticity, so as to vibrate with the filaments of a light that is no longer organized into broad registers, but breaks up into sparks that are like quivers, eating away the forms.
(M. Calvesi, *La realtà del Caravaggio*, 1990)

Essential Bibliography

L'opera completa di Caravaggio, edited by A. Ottino della Chiesa, Milan 1967.

E. Borea, *Caravaggio e i caravaggeschi nelle Gallerie di Firenze*, catalogue of the exhibition at the Uffizi, Florence 1970.

G.A. Dell'Acqua, *Il Caravaggio e le sue grandi opere da San Luigi dei Francesi*, Milan 1971.

Colloquio sul tema Caravaggio e caravaggeschi, booklet no. 5, Accademia Nazionale dei Lincei, Rome 1974.

R. Röttgen, *Il Caravaggio. Ricerche e interpretazioni*, Rome 1974.

Novità sul Caravaggio, Milan 1975.

A. Moir, *Caravaggio and His Copyists*, New York 1976.

B. Nicolson, *The International Caravaggesque Movement. List of Pictures by Caravaggio and his Followers throughout Europe from 1590 to 1650*, Oxford-New York 1979.

R. Longhi, *Caravaggio*, edited by G. Previtali, Rome 1982.

M. Cinotti, G. A. Dell'Acqua, *Michelangelo Merisi detto il Caravaggio. Tutte le opere*, Bergamo 1983.

H. Hibbard, *Caravaggio*, New York 1983.

The Age of Caravaggio, catalogue of the exhibition edited by M. Gregori, New York 1985.

L'ultimo Caravaggio, proceedings of the international convention of studies, Messina 1985 (published in 1987).

M. Marini, *Michelangelo Merisi da Caravaggio "pictor praestantissimus,"* Rome 1987.

Caravaggio. Nuove riflessioni, Rome 1989.

M. Calvesi, *La realtà del Caravaggio*, Turin 1990.